Noon JEWELS Street DOCTOR

DR. JACQUELYN A. WILSON

NOON JEWELS

AN MMOB BOOK

BOOK 1 of PIECES OF ME COLLECTION

Edited/Formatted: Ruthe McDonald
Cover: Barbara McClane
Graphics: Candice J. Kilgore
PR: Tahra Keyes
Style: Dr. Althea Webber Bates
Back cover Photo: Lewis Anthony

ISBN: 978-1-7372391-0-9

MYNDING MY OWN BIZNESS ENTERTAINMENT
With

JOHNRUE™ *PUBLISHING*

PART OF JOHNRUE™ *CREATIVE GROUP, LLC.*

.Dr. Jacquelyn Wilson, Chaplain, Keynote Speaker, Multi-award-winning Film Producer, Celebrity Life-Coach, Business Coach, and Street Doctor, serving the Homeless Community.

Follow Dr. Wilson on Social Media;
FB: @DrWilsom
IG: @OriginalStreetDoctor

Visit her websites:
www.Drjacquelynwilson.com
www.noonjewels.com
www.surprisethestruggling.org
www.thestopbullyingproject.com

For Coaching Services—Personal or Business—
email:
Dr.Wilson@noonjewels.com

Acknowledgements

To my children: There's nothing in this life you cannot do. All that I sacrificed, is for you. I love you and aim for you to live your best life. Never stop dreaming I believe in you.

To my Mentors/Mothers, Iesha Sekou and Glenda Evans for exhibiting greatness to the little girl in me who never had the opportunity to see her mom be all her heart wanted to be—so God introduced her to you guys. Thanks for the tough love, long talks, and guidance. I appreciate you.

To my Connecticut Dream Team! Many thanks and much gratitude to Dr. Althea Bates and Tahra Keyes for your time, selflessness, and love that you have shown and given me. Thanks for working with me…I know it wasn't easy! (LOL)

To my siblings, thank you for being my teachers. Ruthe, Moe, Tim, Trisha—You all have a way of keeping me in my place as the baby. Showing me the dos and don'ts. I have a unique relationship with you all. Thank you for confiding in me and somehow making me the big sister at times! LOL I love you. P.S. Ruthe spoils me most. I'm just saying!

To all the Teen parents, the Homeless youth, the broken battered abused mothers; this is for you. Something you can relate to. A little picker-upper when you need that dose of empowerment. A jewel to get you through the afternoon from a sister who has been where you are. Speaking from experience not TEXT. I'm here to remind you all you have a cheerleader rooting for you. I'm in your corner. I get you. I understand your struggle, that's why I became the woman I once needed.

Darkness has a deadline. Read. Write. Think your way out of your circumstances. Love on you even if all you have is an EBT card. Dress the part. Show up for the King/Queen you're becoming! You got this!

~Your Street Doctor

Dear Reader,

There are individuals who are pretending to have it all together. An act is a part of their daily routine; their covering. Whether emotional, physical, or financial, there is the need to be needed, which helps keeps them together. It numbs them while reminding them, they are alive.

They may not see it, but they are of value to someone even if they don't value themselves. These individuals have forgotten about themselves years ago. They have lost themselves with no self-love, guidance, or tutorials on how to exist in a world that pretends to accept you.

Many were taught to hate who they are and believe that they do not matter. THEY MATTER! It is time to change the dialogue and what they are saying to themselves and about themselves.

Noon Jewels is the first book in the Pieces of Me series; filled with thought-provoking sayings, quotes, and words of wisdom to encourage and inspire you on your journey to standing in and believing your truth, your value, and your power, as Kings and Queens. It is time to adjust your crown.

With Love and Profound Respect,

Dr. Jacquelyn Wilson

Foreward

I have known Dr. Jacquelyn Wilson for some time now. I admired her grind and her work a few years ago when she was promoting her own movie, her company produced, *The Bully.* At the same time, she was also promoting her own artist.

I witnessed the passion she held and it was unmatched by what I was seeing in other people doing the same kind of work. Dr. Wilson stood apart.

Once I met Dr. Wilson, my instincts were right—I always knew she was going to do great things. I also knew, that I had to rub shoulders with her in order for me to level up.

Jerry, Better Known As,
Michael Caldwell

Additional Foreword

There are many things that we will experience throughout our life journey. Some things will leave indelible marks upon our hearts and souls. Scars we will battle against and overcome, if we do not give up on life.

In our journey, God will send people to assist us. I like to call them, Angels in human form. These are individuals that come into your life for a season, and some—if you are so favored of God—for a lifetime.

These individuals encourage us and help us to see God's vision for our life, or remind us of who we are in the eyes of God. They encourage and motivate us. They say things that get us to think. They may also say things that anger us, and push us, but it is all done in love.

We all have different times in our lives when we need to know that someone cares. That, there is more to life than the pain that we have endured. That, there is a purpose for the pain. A purpose for the losses, the hurts, and heartaches. Sometimes we cannot see it, so God will send someone that will say something that will resonate with our hurt and will motivate us, and give validation for what we have been feeling all along.

Noon Jewels is more than a collection of beautiful words and wise sayings. They are words that have been birthed from a place of hurt, disappointments, grief, and heartaches. Dr. Wilson has poured her life, her heart, and experiences onto the pages of this book. Each word, a prose to not only inspire, but also to get one to think.

Maybe you will see yourself in these pages or someone you love, and gain an understanding. Though it may feel like it most of the time, we do not walk this earth alone. There are others here, meant to be a part of our journey. And this season belongs to Dr. Wilson. And if you are reading this, it is your season, also.

Respectfully,

Minister Ruthe McDonald

Dedication

This book is dedicated to my Hero, my BFF, the greatest man to ever live, Arthur M. (Jack) Wilson Sr., for planting seeds in me as a little girl that are now flourishing even in his absence. I love you Daddy. May your soul continue to rest in peace.

To my Mom, Shirleen Wilson. The most beautiful, strongest woman I know. For giving me life. For believing in me, trusting me, praying for me, and always rooting me on. For teaching me the values of giving and non judgment. For inspiring all that I am.
I love you Mommy, this is for you!

To my significant other, Corrie T Minor. I can't believe you're no longer here. I can't believe you're my angel now. I can't believe I'm dedicating this to you. I miss you, I love you. I will continue to raise our children and keep you alive.

To my Angel, Aunt Carrie Maultsby, for being my first cheerleader and prayer warrior. For planting positivity in me all my life. Every conversation. I see the wisdom/vision now. I love you.

To my Ancestors who's shoulders I reside on. To my Grandmothers Roseanna Wilson and Virginia Perez.

NOON JEWELS

—NOON JEWELS—

Queens Don't Trip...

Reflection for this Section: Self-Awareness

As you read through this section of *Noon Jewels*, I ask that you would keep the following questions and statements in mind. This is about self-awareness; how much we know ourselves and what's going on within.

1. How we respond to things is solely our responsibility. We have the power of choice.

2. We can only control our response to what happens to us.

3. It's always the right time to do the right thing.

4. Undecided? Breathe, then make the next right move with your chess piece!

Queens Don't Trip, We Adjust Our Crowns.

The enemy
will try
Anything
to strip you of
Your anointing,
Let him know
you only
Strip for God,
He is my biggest Tipper!

You'd be surprised
By the amount
of people
Who watch you,
Copy you,
Admire your ethic,
But never liked
you!

—NOON JEWELS—

When they can't
change you,
They try
to change
how people
see you.

Quit giving
away your greatness.
When God
gives you the secret
sauce,
It's for you.
Learn to sow in
silence.

—NOON JEWELS—

The moment you realize
Even those who are
supposed to love you,
are the one's hoping
you fail?
Hang in there, buddy!
You'll be hated
in better places
the greater you become.

—NOON JEWELS—

We will never be able to control the actions of others. The only thing we can guarantee control over, is our RESPONSE to their actions.

Some people
Are comfortable
at the bottom.
They don't want
to be saved.

Show up
for you,
Set the tone.
You control
the volume
in your life.

—NOON JEWELS—

Still Under Grace...

Reflection for this Section: Spiritual

As you read through this section of *Noon Jewels*, I ask that you would keep the following questions and statements in mind. This is about your Spiritual healing and nurturing. Be certain to use the journal pages after each *Jewel*, to write down your inner thoughts; things you can come back to, to reflect upon.

1. Grow in your relationship with God! Make Him your everything. Share yourself completely with Him. Confide your darkest intimate secrets. He will cover you and keep you.

2. Are things rocky?

3. Experiencing turbulence?

4. This is the best time to draw nearest to Him. Pour over His word, allowing it to fill you, and all will be well. He is with you. If you believe.

Still under grace,
And
Above the storm.

No one can destroy
you worst
than the people
who are supposed to
love you.
Family is a title.

—NOON JEWELS—

ROOTS, LEAVES, AND BRANCHES

Ask God to reveal to you who the *Roots, Leaves, and Branches* are in your life.

No matter how much we love some people, they will always be a thorny branch. Any association with these branches, brings pain. You can forgive. Take years off. As soon as they're close enough again? They'll prick you. Injecting their venom. Instantaneously leaving you infected. We have to learn to cut these branches for life.

The Leaves are the "*Iffy Mofo's*". They don't know which way to blow. Opportunity controls their loyalty. One minute they love you and need you, the next moment they fall off. You don't see them until the season turns again. They only pop up when in need. They'll betray you. Soon as the weather turns? They blow to the next best opportunity to use someone else.

43

ROOTS, LEAVES, AND BRANCHES…

*…Be mindful…*These are often the closest people to you. Because they're connected to the branches and your roots. They are your siblings, children, parents, family. The people you truly love but they just aren't in your best interest, beloved. They're unstable. They turn colors. They're messy people. They love you until their season of using you is up.

Roots are forever. These are the people God has assigned to you. They are your village. Your community. Your chosen family. They're forever. They grow with you. They water you. Pray with you. Encourage you. Sharpen your iron. They will give you the truth and criticism. They love you for free! They're protective of you. Their loyalty runs deep. There is nothing you could ever do to uproot their love for you.

_____

_____

_____

_____

_____

_____

_____

_____

_____

_____

_____

_____

_____

_____

_____

_____

_____

_____

_____

—NOON JEWELS—

If you're reading this, you're blessed. Don't allow yesterdays sunset to control today's sunrise.

Some of us
wouldn't be
On life support
If we cut the cords
To what's
killing us.

Every rose
comes with
a thorn.
Know what
flowers are
for you!

It is sad...
The ones you sacrifice
for and shared
your loafs with?
Will kill you once you
own the bakery.
Reevaluate whom
you share
bread with.

Internal
warfare is
the
biggest
war!

I don't know who this
is for, but your pain is
about to turn into
glory.
Wipe your eyes
beloved,
your decade of joy,
love, and financial
abundance
is approaching!

—NOON JEWELS—

Know who
you are,
or someone
will tell you
who to be.

Those who are
not for you
Will always
get angered
by you
choosing you!

Sometimes it is that
one person
who has the ability
to nurture in you
what everyone
has failed
to acknowledge.

—NOON JEWELS—

—NOON JEWELS—

Time Doesn't Heal...

Reflection for this Section: The Soul

As you read through this section of *Noon Jewels*, I ask that you would keep the following questions and statements in mind. This is about your Soul and emotional healing and nurturing. Be certain to use the journal pages after each *Jewel*, to write down your inner thoughts; things you can come back to, to reflect upon.

1. Do you feel alone?

2. Do you feel sorry?

3. Are you feeling broken?

4. Understand: It isn't the time that has passed. It's the acceptance of what has broken us. Face your realities, beloved, and allow peace from your acceptance to overrule the emotion. Emotions are a feeling. Let them pass.

Time doesn't
heal all
wounds,
acceptance
does.

—NOON JEWELS—

TIME DOESN'T HEAL ALL WOUNDS ACCEPTANCE DOES!

Once we begin to own our reality, the healing begins. It could be nine months or twenty years. It's all according to the individual. When the student is ready, the teacher (the lesson) arrives. I wish our people knew there's no price tag on peace, self-love, or care. There's no time limit on grief. There's no perfect anything...people are who they are.

People grieve how they grieve.

People love how they've been loved.

People also can be very harsh and quick to judge! In life beloved, when you grow forcefully due to a traumatic experience? When you come from nothing but take the fruits thrown and given and create your own punch? When you work hard? When you teach yourself to save harder? When you Love bigger? When you operate selflessly for years? It changes you. When we recognize peace is everything...we learn to put ourselves first. Don't waste your pain...

TIME DOES NOT HEAL WOUNDS, ACCEPTANCE DOES...

No matter the price. No matter who it affects or whom you have to lose to gain you. I'm in a different space in my life. I'm grieving.

I lost my significant other of fourteen years. I cry a lot. I cry while laughing, eating, driving. Or just gazing. Grief asks no permission. Grief is an invisible elephant.

I know how it feels to be in darkness and mentally alone. At times, I cannot believe my reality today. Death, however, taught me how to live. Once you begin to choose you, your world will change. I can attest to this. All we have is our word, good memories, our karma, and a few assigned beings God may have placed in our lives.

Everyone else will have a need of you. Learn to decipher who's worth your time and who not to allow your heart to beat for any longer. Through it all, you'll learn.

My experiences took acceptance for me to begin healing, not time.

—NOON JEWELS—

TIME DOES NOT HEAL WOUNDS, ACCEPTANCE DOES…

I survived many things: *Homelessness, Domestic violence, Teen pregnancy, Witness to murder, Chemically addicted parents.*
And the list goes on.
The history of a relationship means nothing.
Titles mean nothing.
How one makes you feel is everything!
People can talk you out of many things but, they can never talk you out of how they made you feel. We are all teachers of something. Positive or negative. This life's not about how short we fall, it's about how tall we stand in our beliefs after tripping! All of us have a voice. Share your truths. Own them. Accept them, so when you begin to soar, the remnants of your feathers will free other caged men and women.

71

—NOON JEWELS—

—NOON JEWELS—

I'm not here to play,
I'm here to shake
things up,
be talked about,
like Jesus,
and
Be a vessel
for the Lord.

I was not suppose to be anything... Then God made me everything to somebody!

—NOON JEWELS—

If we—*the world*—
don't know we need
Each other, *NOW.*
By the time we do
know, we won't
Need each other!

You can not
Do business
with selfish people
if you are a giver.
Period!

—NOON JEWELS—

Know your worth
and your why.
You don't have to
attach yourself
to someone
else's dream
for you
to be great!

—NOON JEWELS—

We cannot get
where we are
supposed to be,
If we are poking
holes in the tires
of the vehicle
carrying us!

Blind doesn't mean
you
lack vision.
Without sight,
you become more
in tune with the
things you
cannot see.

When your heart
is too big,
You love too deep
and get screwed
too hard,
By the people
that lingered
too long!

Always know your
Why...
the How?
Will meet you...

Sometimes
we do all we can,
for people who will
never do anything
for us,
just because
we are us.

There's never
a wrong time,
to do the
right thing!

When You Start Putting Yourself First, Healing Has Began and So Do the Hard Choices.

Reflection for this Section: Self-Love

As you read through this section of *Noon Jewels*, I ask that you would keep the following questions and statements in mind. This is about Self-love; healing and nurturing your heart. Be certain to use the journal pages after each *Jewel*, to write down your inner thoughts; things you can come back to, to reflect upon.

1. Does loving yourself come easy or is it something you need to work on?

2. Are you pleased with where you are in life?

3. If you could change anything about yourself, what would it be? Or, do you accept yourself—faults, flaws, and all?

4. When you begin to put yourself first, and take care of your needs before others, that is when healing has began, and making harder choices. What else do you need to work on in the self-love area, if any?

If you see me in
rundown kicks and
old jeans,
I'm doing better
than I look,
I am just investing
in what matters
now.

—NOON JEWELS—

We can never
be anything
we don't
already
believe we are.

Circumstances
do not make
the man.
They merely
reveal him
to himself.

Love is unconditional.
When we love
without judgement,
regardless of
tribulations and trials?
We're loving
God-like.

—NOON JEWELS—

Some people are assigned
to your demise,
They hope you fail.
The moment you begin to
think and do better?
They flee...
It is not in them
to see you healthy
and flourishing.

—NOON JEWELS—

Sparkle
darling.
There's a
diamond
In all of us!

Read Slowly...
Are you breaking
generational
curses?
Or, breaking others
being a curse
to this generation?

—NOON JEWELS—

—NOON JEWELS—

You Are Not Lonely, This Is Your Alone Season.

There will come a time when you'll be stripped of all things, people, and places. All the money in the world couldn't buy you entertainment because, in your heart and mind, you're alone.

There will be moments you'll feel lonely. And in these moments? That is when God is aiming for your attention. It's your allotted creative time. It's your praise and worship time. It's your goal setting and strategizing time.

Zero distractions. All the crutches will be removed until what needs to be deposited is instilled! Your purpose calls for alone seasons, beloved. Embrace it. Where God is about to take you? You're going to need these moments.
This is the best way to learn yourself.
What type of man/woman am I? Do I enjoy myself? My thoughts? My company? Am I datable? Am I whole? Am I ready? Am I serving?

All of the internal rebuilding takes place in your alone season. Don't rush what has slowed down for you, beloved. Pause, Reflect, Destroy
what has to go and build from anew.

Sometimes
you have to
walk away and
just drop the rope.
A war can't be
fought alone.
Let God be
your Mayweather.
1/13/18

—NOON JEWELS—

When you're impregnated with ideas, Don't let the enemy talk you into aborting your dreams.

You ever realize,
You just don't fit
in the circle
you used to twirl in?
You've outgrown it
and don't care to ever
fit in it again!

I don't pretend
to be the best,
I just
guarantee that
I'll always be
Me.

—NOON JEWELS—

Never allow anyone
to tell you,
they didn't know.
Pain is visible
in the eyes.
If they care,
they see it!

Sometimes,
We have to
thank God
for releasing us,
from the
Ropes and Shackles
we've allowed
to keep us bound.

—NOON JEWELS—

If you want
any relationship
of value to last,
Keep your
business between
you and
your trustee!

—NOON JEWELS—

If you're a
part of everything,
you can't be
a part of me.
I don't do
messy people.
Because,
before you know it,
you're in a mix
you cannot fix.

I never changed
my heart.
I just changed
the folk
I allowed it
to beat for.

—NOON JEWELS—

Whatever
feeds your soul,
Chase it down
and keep it on the
MENU...
That is your prey.

—NOON JEWELS—

We will never be
able to control the
actions of others.
The only thing we
can guarantee
control over,
Is our response to
their actions.

They see you
shining,
They just don't
want it
to be you,
Making them
squint!

Grief is a Lonely Place to be, But it's Also a Place of Strengthening.

Reflection for this Section: Gaining Strength

As you read through this section of *Noon Jewels*, I
ask that you would keep the following questions and
statements in mind. This is about gaining strength
while grieving and after grief. Be certain to use the
journal pages after each *Jewel*, to write down your
inner thoughts; things you can come back to, to
reflect upon.

1. Ever felt like it's just YOU? Ever wonder what happened to
   those who said they'd be there after the funeral?

2. When you're facing the grief elephant, who's going to battle it
   with you?

3. Get used to the fact that only God will carry you through this.
   That is TRUTH. And truth is an element of freedom and
   strength.

Love does not
hurt people.
Hurt people
hurt people,
By trying to
love unhealed.

—NOON JEWELS—

LOVE DOES NOT HURT PEOPLE...

On the outside...
Things may seem altogether
Things may seem perfect
Things may seem as though nothing
affects you much...

On the outside, nothing internal is visible
Nothing internal is tangible
Nothing internal is external

On the outside...
You can't see the pain
You can't see a need
You can't witness a broken heart

You can't see the rivers cried due to grief and years of having
it together. Holding others together, while falling apart.
Bursting at the seams. Smiling because it's the right thing to
do. Giving to others, because, it soothes you. Giving so much
that YOU GAVE your ability to make conscious decisions
when it comes to your self-health AWAY....

—NOON JEWELS—

LOVE DOES NOT HURT PEOPLE...

Pain isn't always visible...
The outside of anyone is a shell
Don't be quick to judge a shell.

People are human. Humans have emotions, even if
showing no emotion, is their emotion! This battle is not
mine.

Love doesn't hurt people.
Hurt people hurt people,
by trying to love (unhealed)

On August 22, 2019, I am almost certain I
communicated with God and my Mr. Minor this A.M.,
as we soared through the skies above the clouds and I
witnessed the most beautiful sunrise I saw in my life. It
did something to me and for me. I feel he's at peace.
For once, I'm ok with his death. They assured me that
this is peace. This is heaven. Accept it. He's ok. Move on
to my next chapter so I can be great, and let go of fear.
What Will Be, Will Be.

This is what I came for.

People think
they know you,
Until they finally
meet who you are.
By then,
You're done
knowing them.

Thank you,
For letting me down.
It is because of you,
I know how
to stand up.
I knew
not to await you.
Your word?
Is just something to say
in a sentence.

Don't announce your moves, Just keep moving.

She was too deep for his
shallow mindset.
Every time she would share
a part of herself,
He would drown.
He could never fulfill
his promises.
All he ever did was fail at
what he wanted to pursue,
because he never applied
the action needed.

—NOON JEWELS—

Let nothing
stop you
from
your purpose.
Even if nothing,
is all you've
Got!

I spent
a lot of money
with people
I will
never spend
another moment
with!

—NOON JEWELS—

I don't care
who they are,
Or who they are
connected to.
If the energy
and vibe is off,
We off.

Once
you recognize
your dopeness,
Stop allowing
others to cut it.
Keep them
on lean!

*Always know
who butters
your bread,
And who's
the reason
you never
have any.
Choose your
life fillers wisely.*

Less friends,
less bullshit.
I keep my
circle small.
So small,
All I see is me
most the time...
Shrinkage on a
million!

People will make time
just to copy you,
Monitor whom you
give your seconds
and minutes to.
Everybody can't go
where God
is taking you.
Some have to
hold the door.

If I'm acting
different,
I caught on,
that is all.
No need for long
explanations.

When we allow God
to order our steps,
We're exactly
with whom,
and where
we need to be.

The moment you allow
others to feed you,
You give them
the power
to starve you.
Stay prayed up
and
Motivate yourself.

—NOON JEWELS—

Warning...

Free is the new broke.
Ladies and Gents,
when we don't know our worth,
there will always be a crew
waiting to tell us what we deserve.
People may not make time for you,
but they'll always have time
to tell you who to be
for their benefit.
NOTHING IS FREE...
Your intellectual property has a price.
Charge your PRICE.
Proper Respect (by)Implementing Currency
Exemplary.

Don't whine,
Grind.
Less talk,
More action.
Get to it!

—NOON JEWELS—

Touch her
without
touching her.
That speaks
directly
to her heart.

When
you want to win
as bad as you
want to breathe?
You'll start winning.
You can be anything,
you know that, right?
So why not
start today?

Doesn't matter who you are or what
you've gone through,
We all are teachers of something.
Take the time to learn you.
The part of yourself
that is a world changer.
The part we often ignore
because we know it takes work.
But the rewards are so worth it.
The more we support our employers,
we support their dream.
I'm not saying quit your day job,
I'm saying,
start working on your own vision,
and put that energy into making you
a greater vessel for your purpose.

—NOON JEWELS—

It's who's in our
mirror
that requires
repairing before
we can repair
another...

—NOON JEWELS—

Note to self...

Sometimes we have
to pause from
assisting others
and say,
Look...you going
through your own
Shhhh...

—NOON JEWELS—

Sometimes we're there for so many, we
forget ourselves and
how much we need us,
How to nurture us,
How to love us.
We've become so conditioned
to leaping for others,
that we actually feel bad for putting
ourselves first, in the first place. Something
is wrong.
We have to change
the way we think,
so we can change what we do.
Self-preservation isn't selfish and whomever
doesn't understand, you don't need their
energy no way.

—NOON JEWELS—

Kings and Queens,
it's a new day.
Quit dwelling on
yesterday.
You were blessed
with another day
to start fresh
and plant new seeds.

—NOON JEWELS—

Daddy Issues

Reflection for this Section: Reconciliation

As you read through this section of *Noon Jewels*, I ask that you would keep the following questions and statements in mind. This is about Reconciliation—healing your past, nurturing your future. Be certain to use the journal pages after each *Jewel*, to write down your inner thoughts; things you can come back to, to reflect upon.

1. As a broken fatherless child, you'll have situations arise from your unhealed mini you. How whole would we be, if we had healthy relations with our dads?

2. Would we choose different men?

3. Are we dating father figures?

4. Are our choices in men derived from our lack of a fatherly connection?

5. Men and women suffer from the absence of our heroes. What has dad's disappearance done to me?

Daddy Issues

To the mothers who've lost their
Way. Who's never been
MOTHERED... who's fell to
addiction, abuse,
DADDY Issues.
Who's been struggling, to battle the
demons that have been the vehicle
to your coping mechanisms
Drugs/Sex/Men/Self-sabotage, to
name a few.
To the women who've lost their
children to the system
(Due to such)...

Daddy Issues...

...God told me to tell you; He
forgave you!
God said forgive yourself.
God said those you compare
yourself to?
Are imperfect as well.
They too are battling demons. The
women who are all "*degreed up*",
pretending perfection Via titles,
beauty, possessions, hiding
behind their MASKS...
the one looking down on you?
Who lack accountability,
Are in battle as well.

Daddy Issues...

LADY! Quit counting your losses!
Don't waste your pain another DAY. Work on
YOU. Begin to love you... it's never too late to be
GREAT.
The problem with most of our people? We listen, to
judge. We watch, to tell. We care, with
expectations,
and we love with limits.
The moment we no longer *feel* good, we
immediately separate ourselves from the lesson!
Broken Lady,
Don't be lead by "*feelings*".
Your attitude controls your altitude!
Just know: you're not alone in your pain and you
won't be alone
in your purpose.
It is when we know better,
we can grow better
in *all* relationships in our lives.
Peace and blessings

–NOON JEWELS–

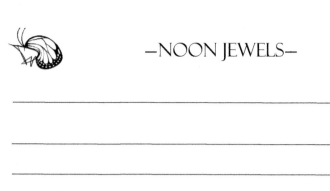

—NOON JEWELS—

Let love
lead you.
Tomorrow isn't
promised.
What people
think of you,
Should never
be your leader.

—NOON JEWELS—

Quit thinking
you know people.
History
hasn't anything
to do with
Evolvement.

—NOON JEWELS—

Sometimes the soul
has a hole so big,
Nothing can fill it up
but God.
Often times we lose ourselves
looking for temporary fillers.
There will come a time
when there's nothing
ANYONE can do for you
but God.
People, places, and things
just aren't enough.
You're going to need God.

When they asked,
"what you're looking at?"
I stared harder.
When my prey got away,
I hunted harder.
And
When the doors I thought were
for me slammed in my face,
I became a carpenter.
I refused to allow anything
sent to destroy me, succeed.
I am the reason I dream.
My experiences are the reason
I take no bull.
My losses, my friends, family, loved ones?
Are the reason I created the cure. Because
nothing makes you sicker than them! ✔

Leap!
God
Will
Catch
You!

Life can change
in the blink
of an eye.
Good news is,
God doesn't blink...
He keeps His eye
on you.

—NOON JEWELS—

Love so hard,
that hate
can't live.
Give so much,
that take
don't exist.

It's nothing
like being
a gift
in the present
moment.

Don't quit your
day dream.
Chase your dreams until
they walk with you
side by side.
Legs are for
dream chasing.
Don't give up.
Your dreams are
counting on you.

I know exactly
who I am,
By learning
exactly who
I'm not.
I fought to
become me.

BE

so beautiful that,
they find beauty
in your ugliness.

Nothing
is easy
until you've
mastered
failing at it.

—NOON JEWELS—

Haters will always be mad,
when they don't hold enough weight
to cut your Dopeness!
She cute, she ready, she self-made,
and she's God's pick.
Just bragging on me,
because I know what it took,
and I know what it still takes.
We must love on ourselves,
because we teach people how to treat us.
It ain't the man, the makeup, or the
clothes... it's the person, the character, the
intentions, the swag, that makes her, *Her.*
Who are you without a man?
A job?
Or your independence?
Money only makes us more
of who we already Are!

—NOON JEWELS—

Losing someone
you love,
is something
you have to
endure
for the rest of
your forever.

Allow folks
to go through
their journey,
Without you
being an
obstacle.

The moment
we open
our mouths,
We introduce
the world
to who
we are.

—NOON JEWELS—

Leaders move
in silence,
And make noise
with the leaders
they create.

—NOON JEWELS—

As long as
you did
the right thing
in any situation,
You can't
go wrong.

Failure
is a major part
of winning.

Align yourself
with people
that make
you happy.

Just when
they thought
they had me
sized up...
I grew a
Notch!

—NOON JEWELS—

I am Breonna Taylor

It's no coincidence we look alike.
Our eyes our hips, the spread of our noses our lips...the
arch in our brows...
The pain that persist.
I didn't have to know her but, she is my sis. We share the
same *OPPRESSORS.* We share the same *THREATS.* We
share the same *HATRED* from others who hate us for our
COLOR. We *RESIDED* IN the same country and drank
milk from the same breast of *Ms. AMERIKKKA,*
the mother of
Slavery. Racism. Blood. Tears. Rape.
Where we are encouraged to abort our wombs, to
assassinate our future *HEROS, KINGS, and QUEENS.*
I am Ms. Taylor!
I am guilty for being innocently black! I am guilty for
sleeping in my bed.
I am not above being
MURDERED WHILE
Eating...Sleeping...Driving...Walking...Wearing a
hoodie...Buying skittles...Selling loosies...
Or CD's while black.

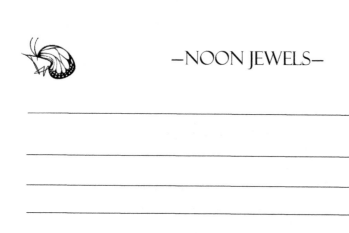

Where God is
taking *you?*
They all can't come,
Beloved.

Someone's got to
tell the tale,
of how they
knew you!

Daily & Nightly Affirmations

7 Things you are grateful For

First, write a letter to your younger self, forgiving those who hurt you and forgiving yourself for hurting yourself. We often underestimate the power of forgiveness.

Make it a daily habit of writing down seven things you are grateful for, when you rise in the morning, and writing seven things you grateful for before you go to rest, in the evening.

This daily exercise will help to shift your thoughts and what you consistently think on through out the day.

Thirty-one Jewels for Thirty Days

A compilation of Jewels to meditate on for 30 days

1. LADIES: It's what's between our ears, not "legs" that matters most.

2. Let nothing get you down even if nothing is all you got!

3. The woman who isn't seeking acceptance/approval is a dangerous woman. The moment you no longer care what anyone thinks? You've gained your wings.

4. Be antisocial when it comes to what God is doing in your life. Social media is a gift and curse. Silence speaks volumes.

5. The sun hit different when you're happy; then the shade get REAL.

6. Your story is the key to another sister's shackles. Share your truth & FREE HER!

7. Whatever fruits you've been THROWN Kings/Queens, create "your juice", sell it, and add taxes.

8. God gives and forgives. Man gets and forgets.

9. The moment we open our mouths we introduce the world to who we are.

10. When we burn bridges, we set ourselves on fire.

11. Don't give too much of your heart to the unstable, they're (guaranteed) to break it.

—NOON JEWELS—

Thirty-one Jewels for Thirty Days

A compilation of Jewels to meditate on for 30 days

12. I woke up so full of love. I'm so grateful to God for the people He has placed and removed out of my life, (because) we become like the people we spend the most time with.

13. Don't be so busy being perfect that you forget to be YOU.

14. A man is only as strong, as the woman behind him.

15. Never pour into someone so much that you fail to fill your cup.

16. We're all one person away. Be ready, and never be the reason they went the other way.

17. Every woman has a lil' girl in her, that still needs her father... it's heartbreaking when he's deceased or (living) like he is.

18. It's an honor to share my story with women in the storm (because) I know how it feels to need an umbrella.

19. You keep going! Don't you ever stop because you aren't validated by the people who're supposed to love you. As long as you got God, you got options.

20. The moment you realize: Even those who are supposed to love you, are the one's hoping you fail? Hang in there buddy. You'll be hated in better places, the greater you become.

21. Always dress the part, beloved. You're being admired whether you get the position or not.

22. Ladies: When he's into you, you won't have to remind him of what you're INTO.

—NOON JEWELS—

Thirty-one Jewels for Thirty Days

A compilation of Jewels to meditate on for 30 days

23. When i die don't post me with no clouds and wings. Post me next to all the lives I inspired and give them two minutes at my HOME GOING.

24. Its the relationships we build that'll bring us over the bridges in life. Sometimes we just have to pause, and thank the Creator for knowledge, wisdom, and understanding. Patience, exposure, and clarity? Are all gifts given.

25. I don't care if it's their last STRAW...Let their BROOMS BREAK!

26. As a child, we do what we're taught. As an adult, we do what we have the will to unlearn.

27. Ladies/Fellas: Love on the one who show's you how important it is for them to not lose you! Love doesn't hurt. Walk in it. Fall for nothing.

28. Best interests is worth more than any amount of money or sex. A person who has your back? Will catch you no matter what you fell from, and not hold it against you because their pleasure is in your GREATNESS.

29. Huge difference between—Telling someone you love them and wanting them to FEEL like you love them.

30. What I know for sure is: I don't need my toxicity leaking on anyone. Our focus should be self healing and far from sexual healing. Everyone wants to RUSH to be loved but, take their time when it comes to building up whom we want to be loved by. Understanding is underrated. While broken homes and marriages, and infidelity are Celebrated.

31. I don't know who needs this but: When you're appointed by the Creator, beloved, the qualifications have been MET! Don't get caught up explaining your elevation! You are who "YOU" are, PERIOD!

—NOON JEWELS—

—NOON JEWELS—

—NOON JEWELS—

—NOON JEWELS—

HARTFORD PUBLIC LIBRARY

500 MAIN STREET

HARTFORD, CT 06103-3075

Made in the USA
Middletown, DE
02 July 2021